GOE/CH

D0192011

TOP OF THE LEAGUE

QED

Publisher: Maxime Boucknooghe
Editorial Director: Victoria Garrard
Art Director: Miranda Snow
Editors: Carly Madden, Claudia Martin
and Sophie Hallam
Design: Mike Henson, Dave Ball
and Angela Ball

First published in the UK in 2016 by
QED Publishing
Part of the The Quarto Group
The Old Brewery
6 Blundell Street
London
N7 9BH

www.qed-publishing.co.uk

A catalogue record for this book is
available from the British Library.

ISBN 978 1 78493 457 6

Printed in China

CONTENTS

LET'S KICK OFF!

Our referee is blowing the whistle. We've lined up the world's greatest players. Fantastic stories and statistics are waiting on the bench. The fans are cheering. So let's kick off with the story of how football began!

A WORLD OF FOOTBALL

Games like football were first played more than 2,000 years ago. The rules may have been different from today's game, but the basic idea was pretty much the same – to play a game of skill and teamwork.

An ancient Greek player shows off some skills.

Europe: At least 2,300 years ago, the ancient Greeks played *episkyros*, a ball game with teams of 12 to 14 men or women. Using the hands was allowed, and so was whacking the other team!

North America: Native Americans enjoyed *pasuckaukohowog*, which means 'they gather to play ball with the foot'. There were up to 500 players on each side. Injuries were standard.

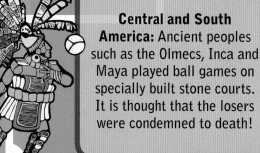

A Sioux Native American team is ready for business, around 1910.

Central and South America: Ancient peoples such as the Olmecs, Inca and Maya played ball games on specially built stone courts. It is thought that the losers were condemned to death!

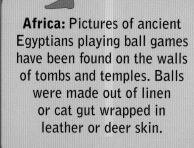

Africa: Pictures of ancient Egyptians playing ball games have been found on the walls of tombs and temples. Balls were made out of linen or cat gut wrapped in leather or deer skin.

Asia: The Chinese were probably the first Asians to play a form of football, over 2,200 years ago. The aim of *cuju* was to kick a feather-filled leather ball into a small net held by bamboo canes.

Oceania: Centuries before the arrival of Europeans, Aboriginal Australians and South Pacific islanders were playing team ball games. In Australia, *marngrook was* played with a coconut as a ball.

Antarctica: The first football match played in Antarctica was in 1914, during an expedition led by explorer Sir Ernest Shackleton.

Players get very chilly in Antarctica, 1914.

TODAY'S TOP TROPHIES

World Cup
The world's greatest football competition kicked off in 1930. It takes place every four years. The first Women's World Cup was held in China in 1991.

Champions League
UEFA launched their new competition – the European Cup – in 1955. It morphed into the Champions League in 1992 and is now the dream cup competition for all Europe's top clubs.

Copa América
This is the oldest international football competition. First held in 1916, it started out with only South American participants, but now two teams from other continents are invited (see page 56).

African Nations Cup
This cup competition has taken place every two years since it began in 1957. The tournament now plays host to around 16 teams from across the continent.

THEN AND NOW

By the 19th century, football had developed into the game we know today. But things were still quite different back then! In the UK, Victorian footballers were unpaid, playing to small local crowds. Today's sporting superstars are millionaires!

↓ PAST ↓

'Handlebar' moustaches were all the rage among 19th-century players.

The first mention of club colours appears in the 'Sheffield Rules' by Sheffield FC in 1857 (before the official rules in 1863!).

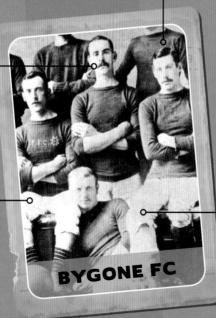

BYGONE FC

Players would often wear cricket whites – many football teams were made up of cricketers keen to play another sport in winter.

Trousers were later cut into shorter 'knickerbockers' for greater ease and agility on the pitch.

THE WHOLE KIT AND CABOODLE

In the mid-19th century, football kits were heavy duty. With woollen shirts and full-length trousers, players struggled in wet weather. Football kits are now made from lightweight, artificial fibres in club colours. Today's footballing *fashionistas* are on the ball with style trends, showcasing their experimental hairstyles and eye-catching tattoos on the pitch.

↓ PRESENT ↓

The names of club sponsors stand out on today's shirts to maximize publicity.

Real Madrid super-striker Cristiano Ronaldo is a good example of today's world-famous celebrity players. He wears personalized football boots and signs mega sponsorship deals.

RONALDO

The club's home and away kits are instantly recognizable to fans.

SOME EARLY REFEREES WERE REAL SMARTY-PANTS ON THE PITCH, OPTING FOR FORMAL TROUSERS, BLAZERS AND BOW TIES!

RONALDO HAS OPENED UP A PUBLIC MUSEUM, DEDICATED TO HIMSELF!

SUPER SIGNINGS

In 1905, the first £1,000 transfer took place when Sunderland's **Alf Common** joined Middlesbrough. More than a century later, in 2013, Tottenham's **Gareth Bale** signed for Real Madrid for £85 million, making him the most expensive player of all time.

ON THE MOVE

Many European players were on the move following the Bosman Ruling of 1995, which stated that players could transfer to a new team when their contracts ran out – without their previous club receiving a fee – and each team could feature more than three foreign players from the European Union.

PLAYING BY THE RULES

Before the 19th century, different football teams played by different rules. The rows must have got heated!

1863
The Football Association (FA) was formed in England. It is the sport's first governing body. The first official rules were set down.

1904
The Fédération Internationale de Football Association (FIFA) is founded in Paris. It oversees international matches, which must be played by the rules of the International Football Association Board.

1970s
Referees start limiting bad behaviour on the field by handing out yellow cards. A red card (or two yellows) means a player can be sent off for an early bath.

MONEY, MONEY, MONEY

In the 19th century, players came to the football field from all walks of life. The game offered little financial reward, so everyday work was essential. Until the 1960s, the top wage for a player was just £20 per week. Professional players in today's top leagues are multi-millionaires, many of whom earn even more money from advertising and sponsorship deals. With all this wealth to spare, many players give back to the wider community. For example, **Ronaldo** donated £5 million to help those affected by the Nepal earthquake of 2015.

SUPER STADIUMS

As football continued to win new fans, the growing crowds needed somewhere to watch their favourite game. In the late 19th century, the first specially built football grounds appeared, with stands for spectators. Today, the world's top clubs play at state-of-the-art stadiums with undersoil heating and covered seating for tens of thousands of fans.

BIGGER AND BETTER

The biggest stadium in football history was the **Maracanã** in Rio de Janeiro, Brazil. It once held 200,000 people, but its capacity was cut to nearly 80,000 for safety reasons. Today's biggest ground is North Korea's **Rungrado May Day Stadium**, which has room for 150,000 supporters to watch the national football team. The largest club stadium is the stunning **Camp Nou** in Spain, where Barcelona play their home games in front of nearly 100,000 people. The stands are scarily steep and high, which creates an incredible atmosphere for both the home and away supporters.

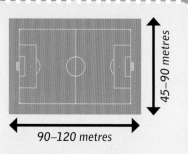

45–90 metres

90–120 metres

SIZE MATTERS

Football laws allow some differences in the size of pitches. These differences can sometimes affect the game. For example, attacking teams going broad and deep may do well in wider spaces. Tighter, defensive teams can use small or narrow spaces better.

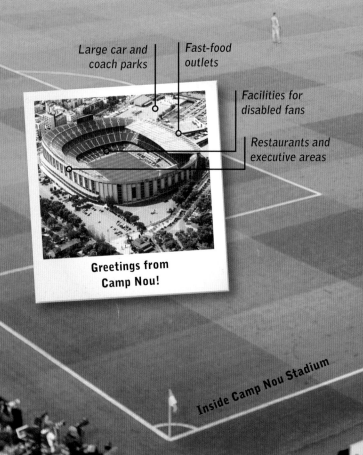

Large car and coach parks

Fast-food outlets

Facilities for disabled fans

Restaurants and executive areas

Greetings from Camp Nou!

Inside Camp Nou Stadium

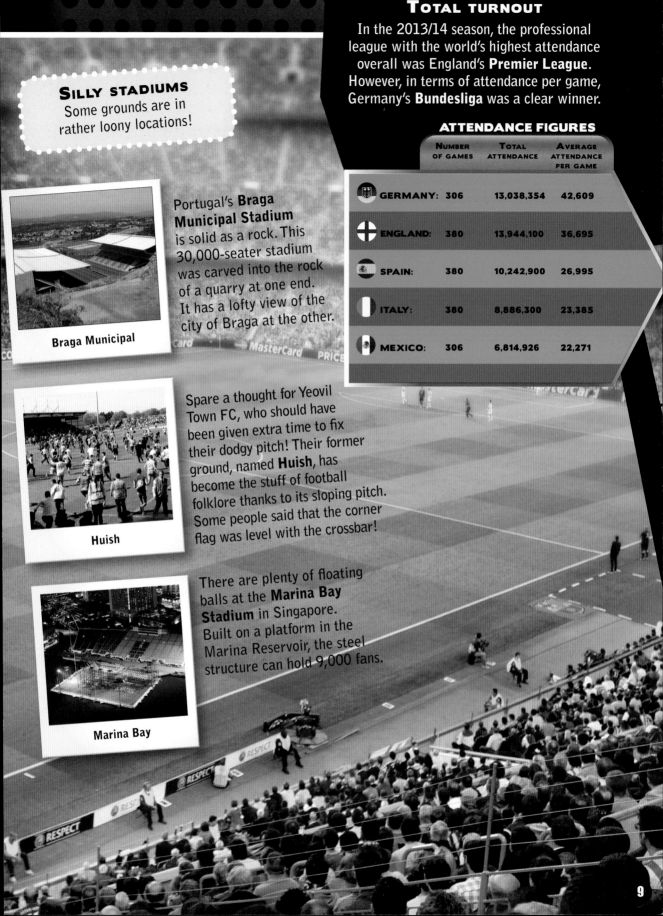

In the 2013/14 season, the professional league with the world's highest attendance overall was England's **Premier League**. However, in terms of attendance per game, Germany's **Bundesliga** was a clear winner.

SILLY STADIUMS

Some grounds are in rather loony locations!

Portugal's **Braga Municipal Stadium** is solid as a rock. This 30,000-seater stadium was carved into the rock of a quarry at one end. It has a lofty view of the city of Braga at the other.

Braga Municipal

ATTENDANCE FIGURES

	NUMBER OF GAMES	TOTAL ATTENDANCE	AVERAGE ATTENDANCE PER GAME
GERMANY:	306	13,038,354	42,609
ENGLAND:	380	13,944,100	36,695
SPAIN:	380	10,242,900	26,995
ITALY:	380	8,886,300	23,385
MEXICO:	306	6,814,926	22,271

Spare a thought for Yeovil Town FC, who should have been given extra time to fix their dodgy pitch! Their former ground, named **Huish**, has become the stuff of football folklore thanks to its sloping pitch. Some people said that the corner flag was level with the crossbar!

Huish

There are plenty of floating balls at the **Marina Bay Stadium** in Singapore. Built on a platform in the Marina Reservoir, the steel structure can hold 9,000 fans.

Marina Bay

CLUB CORNER
PART ONE: KINGS OF EUROPE

Europe is home to the world's most celebrated leagues. Here's a look at some of the best clubs in Europe's 'Big Five': England's Premier League, Spain's La Liga, Germany's Bundesliga, France's Ligue 1 and Italy's Serie A.

ENGLAND'S PREMIER LEAGUE

LIVERPOOL FC
'THE REDS'

TROPHY CABINET
5 EUROPEAN CUP (CHAMPIONS LEAGUE) TITLES
3 UEFA CUP (EUROPA LEAGUE) TITLES
3 UEFA SUPER CUPS
18 LEAGUE CHAMPIONSHIPS
7 FA CUPS
8 LEAGUE CUPS
15 CHARITY OR COMMUNITY SHIELDS

In 1901, Liverpool FC won its first league title. The team then won five league titles in the first half of the 20th century. But it was manager **Bill Shankly** who changed the club's fortunes from 1959–1974. Liverpool became a giant of English football and won its first European title in 1977. It won the European Cup again in 1978, 1981, 1984 and 2005. Surprisingly for such a big club, Liverpool hasn't won the English league since 1990.

SPAIN'S LA LIGA

Originally named Madrid FC in 1902, the club was given the name Real (meaning Royal) in 1920, by King Alfonso XIII of Spain. FIFA chose Real Madrid as the Best Club of the 20th Century – and you only have to look at its trophy cabinet to work out why. The team won the first five European Cups. The club is owned by its members and has had the highest income in the world over the last ten years.

REAL MADRID
'LOS BLANCOS (THE WHITES)'

TROPHY CABINET
FIFA's BEST CLUB OF THE 20TH CENTURY
10 EUROPEAN CUP (CHAMPIONS LEAGUE) TITLES
2 UEFA CUP (EUROPA LEAGUE) TITLES
2 INTERCONTINENTAL CUPS
1 FIFA CLUB WORLD CUP
2 UEFA SUPER CUPS
32 SPANISH CHAMPIONSHIPS
19 COPA DEL REY TITLES
9 SPANISH SUPER CUPS
1 SPANISH LEAGUE CUP

BAYERN MUNICH

'DIE BAYERN (THE BAVARIANS)'

TROPHY CABINET
5 EUROPEAN CUP (CHAMPIONS LEAGUE) TITLES
1 UEFA CUP (EUROPA LEAGUE) TITLE
1 EUROPEAN CUP WINNERS' CUP
2 INTERCONTINENTAL CUPS
1 FIFA CLUB WORLD CUP
1 UEFA SUPER CUP
25 GERMAN CHAMPIONSHIPS
14 GERMAN CUPS
4 GERMAN SUPER CUPS
6 GERMAN LEAGUE CUPS

Founded in 1900, Bayern Munich is Germany's most successful team, with nearly 50 German trophies in the bag. Three of its five European Cups came one year after another in the 1970s. Some of Germany's most famous names have played for the side, including **Franz Beckenbauer**, **Gerd Müller** and **Philipp Lahm.**

With its huge army of fans, Marseille regularly gets the highest attendance in France. Established in 1899, the club has led the league in French football, spending most seasons in Ligue 1. It has topped the league nine times and broken records by grabbing the Coupe de France ten times. The team won the European Cup in 1993.

OLYMPIQUE DE MARSEILLE

'LES PHOCÉENS (THE PEOPLE OF MARSEILLE)', 'L'OM' OR 'LES OLYMPIENS (THE OLYMPIANS)'

TROPHY CABINET
1 EUROPEAN CUP (CHAMPIONS LEAGUE) TITLE
9 FRENCH LEAGUE TITLES
10 COUPES DE FRANCE
3 FRENCH SUPER CUPS
3 FRENCH LEAGUE CUPS

JUVENTUS

'LA VECCHIA SIGNORA (THE OLD LADY) OF TURIN' OR 'THE ZEBRAS'

TROPHY CABINET
2 EUROPEAN CUP (CHAMPIONS LEAGUE) TITLES
1 EUROPEAN CUP WINNERS' CUP
1 UEFA CUP (EUROPA LEAGUE) TITLE
2 EUROPEAN SUPER CUPS
2 INTERCONTINENTAL CUPS
31 SERIE A LEAGUE TITLES
10 COPPA ITALIA TROPHIES
6 ITALIAN SUPER CUPS

Formed in 1897, Juventus is Italy's best-supported club. Its famous black-and-white striped shirts actually come from an English team. When a club member asked a friend in England to send shirts for the newly formed Juventus, the Notts County fan sent replicas of his team's shirts!

CLUB CORNER
PART TWO: GLOBAL GIANTS

Here are some more giants of the game, playing across Europe and the rest of the world. One of these giants is sadly no longer with us, but the rest are still winning silverware and strong support.

NETHERLANDS
AFC AJAX

- 4 EUROPEAN CUP (CHAMPIONS LEAGUE) TITLES
- 1 EUROPEAN CUP WINNERS' CUP
- 33 DUTCH LEAGUE TITLES • 1 UEFA CUP
- 18 KNVB CUPS • 1 UEFA SUPER CUP

Named after an ancient Greek hero, Ajax has four Champions League titles under its belt. The team has been known for its system of 'total football', passing the ball so quickly that any player could score.

NORTH AMERICA

EURO

AFRIC

SOUTH AMERICA

UNITED STATES
NEW YORK COSMOS

- 5 NORTH AMERICAN LEAGUE TITLES
- 2 TRANSATLANTIC CHALLENGE CUPS

New York Cosmos was part of an exciting but – in the end – unsuccessful attempt to have a football league in the USA. The North American Soccer League ran from 1968 to 1984. Cosmos started in 1970, quickly drawing A-list players like the legendary **Pelé**. Sadly the club closed in 1985.

ARGENTINA
CA BOCA JUNIORS

- 3 INTERCONTINENTAL CUPS • 6 COPA LIBERTADORES
- 2 COPA SUDAMERICANA • 5 RECOPA SUPER CUPS SUDAMERICANA
- 23 NATIONAL LEAGUE TITLES • 2 NATIONAL CUPS

A group of young men from Genoa, in Italy, founded Boca Juniors in 1905. This is now the most popular club in Argentina, with 40 per cent of the population saying they are fans. Among the great players to wear their shirts were **Carlos Tevez** and **Diego Maradona**.

PORTUGAL
SL BENFICA (SLB)

- 2 EUROPEAN CUP (CHAMPIONS LEAGUE) TITLES
- 5 UEFA CUP (EUROPA LEAGUES) TITLES
- 34 PRIMEIRA LIGA TITLES
- 25 PORTUGUESE CUPS
- 6 PORTUGUESE LEAGUE CUPS
- 5 PORTUGUESE SUPER CUPS

Along with Sporting Lisbon and Porto, Benfica is one of the big three clubs in Portugal. Founded in 1904, the club enjoyed super success in the 1960s. They were European champions in 1961 and 1962, triumphing over first Barcelona and then Real Madrid.

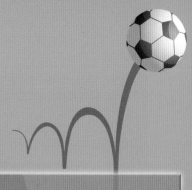

EGYPT
AL AHLY SC

- **37** League titles
- **35** Egyptian Cups
- **8** Egyptian Super Cups
- **8** African Champions League titles
- **1** Confederation Cup
- **4** African Cup Winners' Cups
- **6** African Super Cups
- **1** Arab Champions Cup
- **1** Arab Cup Winners' Cup
- **2** Arab Super Cups
- **1** Afro-Asian Cup

Egypt was under British rule in 1900 when anti-British students set up Al Ahly in the capital city of Cairo. The Egyptian league got under way in 1948, with Al Ahly taking the first ten championships! The club still dominates the nation's football and often plays in the FIFA Club World Cup.

ASIA

JAPAN
KASHIMA ANTLERS

- **7** J. League titles
- **4** Emperor's Cups
- **5** Japanese League Cups
- **5** Japanese Super Cups
- **1** A3 Champions' Cup

The club first formed in 1947, but the Kashima ('Deer Island') Antlers only became Japan's biggest success story when the professional J. League started in 1993. In 2000, the team won the hat-trick, taking all three major Japanese titles for the first time.

AUSTRALIA
MELBOURNE VICTORY FC

- **3** A-League titles
- **3** A-League Finals
- **1** A-League Pre-Season Challenge titles

The club was founded in 2004, the same year as Australia's national league. Victory is the most popular team in Oz, drawing crowds of up to 25,000 fans. The top scorer is **Archie Thompson**, who was the club's first ever signing. Victory has come top of the A-League three times, making them the nation's most successful team.

SOUTH AFRICA
ORLANDO PIRATES FC

- **4** Premier Soccer League titles
- **1** National Soccer League title
- **4** National Premier Soccer League titles
- **8** Nedbank Cups • **1** Telekom Knockout title
- **9** MTN 8 Cups • **1** CAF Champions League title
- **1** CAF Super Cup

A few teenagers set up the Orlando Pirates in 1934. South Africa's Premier Soccer League formed in 1996, with the Pirates the only club to stay in the top league ever since. They are the only South African team to have won the African Champions League.

THE DREAM TEAM

Football has produced some incredibly skilled players from all over the planet, so it's hard to squeeze them down to just 11 'dream' footballers. This dream team features a selection of the game's true greats – but if you've got your own favourites, bring them on as substitutes!

FRANZ BECKENBAUER

DEFENDER

This incredibly skilful German defender scored more than 70 goals for Bayern Munich. He was the first footballer to win the World Cup as a player (in 1974) and then win it again as a manager (in 1990).

KRISTINE LILLY

MIDFIELDER

From 1987 to 2010, Lilly appeared 352 times for the all-conquering US women's national team and scored 130 goals, many from midfield. She also has a full trophy cabinet, winning two World Cups and two Olympic gold medals.

LUÍS FIGO

WINGER

Figo enjoyed a starry career at club level with Sporting Lisbon, Barcelona, Real Madrid and Inter Milan. He bagged many trophies, including the FIFA World Player of the Year in 2001. He also put in 127 appearances for Portugal, scoring 34 times.

JOHAN CRUYFF

MIDFIELDER

Dutch midfielder Cruyff won European Footballer of the Year three times in the 1970s, and lifted three European Cups with Ajax. He enjoyed success at Barcelona and returned to manage them in 1989, taking four league titles and a European Cup. In 48 international games, he found the back of the net 33 times.

LIONEL MESSI

FORWARD

Tormenting defenders with his super skills, Messi scored 73 goals in a single season (2011–12) and has bagged more than 400 goals for his club, Barcelona. In 2012–13, he scored in 21 Spanish league games in a row – another record. He was named as the World Cup's best player in 2014.

LEV YASHIN

Believed to have saved more than 100 penalties, Yashin's safe hands helped his club Dynamo Moscow to win five Soviet league titles. He won an Olympic football gold medal in 1956. He remains the only keeper ever to have won the European Footballer of the Year award.

BOBBY MOORE

Moore was England captain the only time the team won the World Cup, in 1966. He was one of the world's best defenders – according to Pelé, he was the greatest defender he ever played against. Moore debuted for West Ham aged 17 in 1958, and played 642 games for them.

PAOLO MALDINI

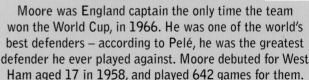

The outstanding Italian defender first played for AC Milan in 1985 and continued to play for them for 25 seasons! He won seven Italian league titles, five European Cups (now known as Champions League titles) and also played for Italy 125 times.

GEORGE BEST

This gifted Northern Ireland winger was so skilful that he held off defenders with ease. From 1963 to 1974, he appeared 470 times for Manchester United and scored 179 goals. He was also one of the first celebrity footballers and was nicknamed the 'Fifth Beatle', after the world's biggest pop group of the 1960s and '70s.

MARTA

At just 1.6 metres tall, Marta is small for a footballer, but she packs a powerful punch, averaging more than a goal a game for Brazil. She has been voted World Player of the Year a record-breaking five times (2006–10) and was runner-up three times.

PELÉ (CAPTAIN)

The Brazilian legend played for his club, Santos, at 15, his country at 16, and at 17 became the youngest goal-scorer at a World Cup – a competition he would win three times (1958, 1962 and 1970). This goal machine remains the top scorer for both Brazil and Santos – with 77 goals for his country and over 1,200 for his team.

NIGHTMARE UNITED

Forget dream teams! It's more like a nightmare for some players. A bad run of games or a nasty injury can affect the rest of the team. But a howler in a big match can mean disaster for the club. Check out this line-up of bunglers whose mistakes, miskicks and mishaps were all too costly.

STEVIE'S SLIP

In the race for the 2014 English Premier League title, Liverpool's **Steven Gerrard** slipped during a Chelsea attack on goal, allowing **Demba Ba** to score. Liverpool lost 2–0, pushing them out of the race and letting Manchester City triumph.

POOR PENALTIES

Argentina's **Martín Palermo** is in the record books for all the wrong reasons. During the Copa América of 1999, the supposed striker missed three penalties against Colombia in a match that haunted his career.

SPRAIN PAIN

When Brazilian forward **Maurides Roque Junior** scored for the first time while playing for Porto Alegre's Internacional SC in 2013, he somersaulted with joy! Unfortunately, he sprained his knee in the process and didn't play for nearly a year.

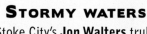

STORMY WATERS

Stoke City's **Jon Walters** truly had a bad game against Chelsea in 2013. After two own goals, a penalty miss, and a 4–0 defeat, it's a match he'll want to forget! He'll find that hard, as it is often named as the worst performance in Premier League history.

A WHIFF OF WOE

The sweet smell of success was smashed to smithereens when Spain's first-choice goalie, **Santiago Cañizares**, dropped a bottle of aftershave on his foot in 2002. Suffering a severed tendon, the careless keeper missed the entire World Cup.

DUTCH DISASTER

Despite plenty of chances, Dutchman **Pascal Bosschaart** was goalless in nearly 400 games for Utrecht, Feyenoord and Sydney. He even managed to miss a penalty in his final game for Utrecht.

SLIP OF THE TONGUE

Blink and you'd miss Cross Farm striker **Lee Todd**'s appearance in a UK Sunday league match in 2000. When the referee blew the whistle – loudly – for kick-off, the surprised striker said a 'naughty' word. He was given a red card – after just two seconds on the pitch!

BACK TO BED

Real Salt Lake's **Fabián Espíndola** celebrated in style after scoring in 2008. Following a daredevil backflip, he hurt his ankle and was out of action for two months. To add insult to injury, his goal was offside and disallowed anyway.

CALAMITY JAMES

Goalkeeper **David James** made some cracking saves, but the FA Cup final saw some of his biggest blunders! As Liverpool goalie in 1996, he punched the ball to Manchester United's **Eric Cantona** to score the winner. As Aston Villa goalie in 2000, he gave the ball to Chelsea's **Roberto Di Matteo** to do exactly the same.

OWN-GOAL MAESTRO

Nigerian-born **Festus Baise** was keen to show off his moves for Sun Hei, in the Hong Kong league, in 2011. Unleashing a reverse scorpion kick, his stunning effort flew past the keeper and straight into his own net.

BROKEN BRAZIL

A special mention must go to the entire Brazil team for their performance against Germany in the 2014 World Cup semi-final. When these two giants met, everyone expected a closely fought battle. Instead, the Brazilians were 5–0 down by half-time, with four goals during a devastating six minutes. They ended up losing 7–1 to the future World Cup winners.

GIANT-KILLERS

Against all odds, some teensy little football clubs have beaten the game's giants, slaying them with shocking scorelines that no one predicted. But these cup upsets or league game unsettlers can actually help the sport – by boosting player confidence, getting everyone talking, and building on football's memorable history.

OOOH-LA-LA!

Picture the scene. It's the French Cup final in the year 2000. Who might be playing? Maybe Paris Saint-Germain or Marseille. But no. The big fish were off the menu – the minnows were in action. Amateur side Calais reached the final, with their team of gardeners, shop assistants and ferry workers. They beat Bordeaux 3–1 in the semi-finals but were finally defeated by Nantes. Calais became the first amateur side to be in the French Cup final in 82 years of the competition.

CAMEROON'S CONQUERORS

The 1990 World Cup finals got off to a cracking start when Cameroon took on the world champions, Argentina, who boasted legend **Diego Maradona** in their line-up. But this gave Cameroon nothing to lose. In a feisty match, with 30 bookings, **François Omam-Biyik** of Cameroon headed in the only goal, making the African underdogs victorious.

CALAIS : 3
VS
BORDEAUX : 1

ITALIAN DREAM

At the top of the Italian football league, you'll usually find the clubs of major cities, such as AC and Inter Milan, Roma and Juventus. But in 1985, little-known Hellas Verona won the Serie A league title for the first and only time. Winning the league is even trickier than a cup competition, because teams need to get results week in, week out. Hellas Verona beat big names including Torino, Juventus and Udinese to end up on top.

Verona

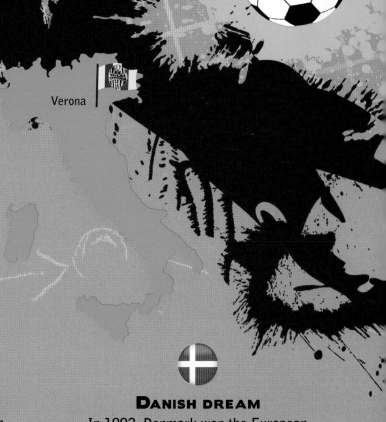

CURSE OF THE CUP

The FA Cup has proved to be a problem for many of England's greats over the years. Manchester United got that sinking feeling when they lost 2–0 to seasiders Bournemouth in 1984. Arsenal has come a cropper several times, losing to Walsall in 1933, York in 1985 and Wrexham in 1992. Chelsea also suffered a huge upset in 2015, when Bradford came from 2–0 down to win 4–2 at Stamford Bridge.

DANISH DREAM

In 1992, Denmark won the European Championship against all odds. The team was given only a week's notice to prepare a squad for the competition after Yugoslavia were excluded due to their country's civil war. The Danes had finished runners-up to Yugoslavia in the group stages. The Danes competed in the tournament with seven other nations and ended up winners, beating Germany 2–0 in the final.

1984
BOURNEMOUTH 2–0 MANCHESTER UNITED

1992
WREXHAM 2–1 ARSENAL

2015
CHELSEA 2–4 BRADFORD

DANMARK EUROPA MESTER I 3.75
Nordfoto/Ole Knappe del. 1992

A NUMBERS GAME...

Numbers, statistics and scores pile up in a football game, with minutes of play and formations such as 4-4-2 and 3-5-1-1. But some facts and figures are exciting because they are extraordinary, giving fans something to really cheer about.

SAUSAGE SUM

Romanian football club Regal Hornia gave 15 kilograms of pork sausages to buy Romanian defender **Marius Cioara** in 2006. Cioara was so upset by being swapped for sausages that he quit football the very next day.

SPEEDIEST SHOT

Sporting Lisbon's **Ronny Heberson** kicked a flying free kick during a 2006 Portuguese league match at a speed of 211 kilometres per hour. This was the fastest-known shot in football, nearing the average speed of a Formula 1 racing car.

TEENAGE KICKS

Midfield maestro **Freddy Adu** was only 14 when he scored his first goal in Major League Soccer for DC United. He is the youngest-ever goal-scorer in major-league professional football.

92

HAT-TRICK HERO

Brazilian striker **Pelé** has scored a hat-trick (three goals) 92 times!

Greetings from...

'Isles of Scilly

LITTLE LEAGUE

There are two teams in the world's smallest league! Woolpack Wanderers and Garrison Gunners make up the Isles of Scilly League. The rivals play each other 18 times every season and compete in two cup competitions.

NAMES AND NUMBERS

The Number 1 jersey is often worn by the goalkeeper but during the 1978 World Cup, goalie **Ubaldo Fillol** wore the number 5 jersey. His Argentinian team were given shirt numbers based on the alphabetical order of their names. Although midfielder **Norberto Alonso** got the number 1 shirt, Ubaldo Fillol was voted the best goalie of the tournament!

SUPER SCORELINE

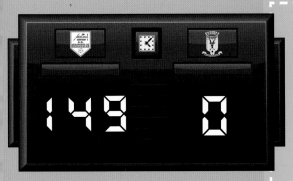

149–0 is the highest-known score in a competitive football match. It occurred in 2002 during the THB Champions League in Madagascar. An argument between two top teams turned ugly when the Stade Olympique l'Emyrne team staged a revolt by scoring own goals. After each own goal, the SO l'Emyrne players got the ball back to restart the game. Opponents AS Adema were powerless to stop them scoring again and again... and again!

LAST FAN STANDING

One lone Udinese fan turned up for a 2012–13 Serie A match against Sampdoria in Genoa, Italy. The fan, named Arrigo Brovedani, was initially booed by the 20,000 home fans, but was later given drinks and a free shirt by the home club. His team's 2–0 away win only added to his solo celebrations!

SWIFT STRIKE

Turkey's **Hakan Sükür** took 11 seconds after kick-off to score against South Korea in the 2002 World Cup. It remains the competition's fastest goal.

57.3 m

HEAD START

Jone Samuelsen's header flew 57.3 metres – the longest distance of any headed goal. Samuelsen was playing for Norwegian team Odd Grenland in 2011, when he headed the ball from his own half and watched it reach the back of Tromsø IL's net. He nods, he scores!

Breathable football shirts, sponsored neon boots and rubber balls are all part and parcel of today's game. But back in the 19th century, players struggled with weighty woollen shirts, bulky boots – and a pig's bladder to kick around!

1860

SWEATING IT OUT
• 1860s •

The earliest uniform kits had heavy woollen or cotton long-sleeved shirts. Players built up a sweat in them, with the fibres getting even heavier in rain. Kits also included full-length trousers, but there were no shin pads to protect against the chunky boots of the opposition.

19 40

PUT THE BOOT IN
• 1940s •

Teams in South America introduced light, low-cut boots that were more comfortable and safer to wear. This style was soon adopted across Europe. By the 1950s, the black-and-white boot was brought in, a look still in favour today. Studs moved from leather and rubber to today's plastic or metal screw-ins.

1910

SOGGY BALLS • 1870s •

Some of the earliest footballs were inflated pig bladders. Later, animal hides were cured (hardened) into leather for balls. By the 1870s, balls were often made of eight pieces of unprotected leather stitched together. They got heavy and soggy when it rained!

1870

UNDER YOUR HAT • 1910s •

In the late 19th century, early female teams covered their legs in whopping bloomers. During World War I (1914–18), with most men away fighting, women's football became very popular. Although they now wore lighter shorts, the players had to cover their hair with caps.

1950

Manchester United 1955-56

LASER BOOTS • 2000s •

Today's boots are super lightweight and styled to improve the player's stability and contact with the ball. The big players wear new boots for every game, often designed especially for them with personalized details and striking neon colours. Boots can be moulded exactly for the player's feet using lasers. Sponsored stars receive huge sums of money to wear company-branded boots.

FABULOUS FIBRES • 1950s •

Players breathed a sigh of relief when football shirts and socks made with man-made fibres were introduced from the 1950s. Fibres such as polyester were a life-saver, keeping the wearer cool and cutting down on sweat. Shorts had also become shorter and lighter, making it easier for players to move.

2000

ARTIFICIAL WORKS OF ART • 1998 •

Today, nearly half the world's footballs are made in the Sialkot area of Pakistan. They are crafted from man-made materials such as polyurethane and have a waterproof coating. Handheld pumps are used to inflate the balls to the correct pressure. Traditional black-and-white balls were replaced by coloured versions – for the first time – at the 1998 World Cup (held in France).

1998

WOMEN AT THE FRONT • 2015 •

As enthusiasm for the female game grew, women's kits developed alongside men's. Caps were ditched in favour of long hair being tied back. Today's players are completely up to speed with modern kits, made up of lightweight, high-tech materials for shirts, shorts and socks as seen at the 2015 Women's World Cup finals (held in Canada).

2015

Football would be nothing without the fans. Supporters of the game are fiercely loyal – they wear their club colours, sing their side's songs, and follow their teams to home and away fixtures. This passion and pride has made football the most watched sport in the world.

BONKERS FOR BRAZIL

The most fanatical supporter of Brazil is probably Nelson Paviotti. Since Brazil won the World Cup in 1994, he has only worn colours featured on the national flag (yellow, green, white and blue). To honour the 2014 World Cup taking place in Brazil, he covered his home in the Brazilian colours. In fact, Brazil's fans were some of the first to paint their faces and play drums and whistles, creating a carnival atmosphere inside their home grounds.

KNOCKOUT MATCH

During a Euro 2008 qualifier, Denmark fought back from 3–0 to 3–3 against Sweden. But disaster struck in the 89th minute when a Danish player was sent off for throwing a punch. A Danish spectator invaded the pitch and swung his own fist at the referee, who then called the game off. A 3–0 win was later awarded to Sweden. The Swedes were pleased as punch, heading off to the tournament finals, while Denmark missed out.

AS EASY AS IT LOOKS...?

West Ham United fan Steve Davies was moaning at the strikers from the stands during a pre-season friendly, in 1994, when assistant boss **Harry Redknapp** overheard him. Redknapp pulled him out of the crowd and sent him down the tunnel. Davies soon came out wearing the club kit. He was given half an hour to show if he could do any better up front. According to football folklore, Davies even scored a goal!

CHEEKY CHAP

There was an unfamiliar face in the team shot taken before the Champions League match between Manchester United and Bayern Munich in 2001. Lining up alongside legends such as **Giggs**, **Keane** and **Scholes** was… Karl Power. This cheeky chap donned United's away kit, nipped past security at the German ground and took his place for the official pre-match photo. Definitely one for the album.

LONG-DISTANCE LEAGUE

The travel bills for USA's Major League Soccer fans must be huge. When supporters of the Portland Timbers go to New York, it is the same distance as London to Baghdad. LA Galaxy visiting Boston is a longer ride than travelling from Tokyo in Japan to the Philippines.

NAME GAME

Some football fans have named their newborn babies after a preferred club or player. Just ask Zinedine Yazid Zidane Thierry Henry Barthez Eric Felipe Silva Santos! This Brazilian boy was named after the French football stars of the 2006 World Cup, because his father was so impressed by their winning performances.

ALL-ROUND APPRECIATION

In 2003, Brazilian striker **Ronaldo** scored a hat-trick during his team Real Madrid's 4–3 win over Manchester United. He got a standing ovation from the United fans. A year later, French forward **Thierry Henry** gave a football masterclass during Arsenal's 5–1 win over Portsmouth. Even the Portsmouth fans cheered his skills. Past rivalries were forgotten when **Ronaldinho** scored two goals for Barcelona against Real Madrid in 2005. The Real fans applauded the striker's show-stopping performance.

SUPER SUPREMOS

The success or failure of a team is often down to the manager. It's all about his or her match-day team selection and tactics, as well as how they motivate the players. It's hard to narrow down football's best managers, but here are some of the top dogs...

FLYING SCOTSMAN

Sir Alex Ferguson managed Manchester United from 1986 to 2013. It was the most successful team in Premier League history, winning every competition going. His trophy cabinet was bursting with three Premier League titles, five FA Cups, four League Cups and two Champions League titles. Phew!

PORTUGUESE PRODIGY

José Mourinho calls himself the 'Special One'. Although he is lacking in modesty, he may have a point. He is the only manager to win the league with four different clubs in four different leagues in four different countries – Porto (Portugal), Chelsea (England), Inter Milan (Italy) and Real Madrid (Spain).

Sir Alex Ferguson

José Mourinho

Pep Guardiola

WINNING WONDER

Spanish star **Pep Guardiola** always had that winning feeling. During the four years he managed Barcelona, he sneaked 14 trophies under his belt. In 2013, he took over at Bayern Munich and swiftly set about winning yet more trophies.

SHARED SUCCESS

Brazil's **Mário Zagallo** and Germany's **Franz Beckenbauer** are the only men to have won the World Cup for their home countries as both players and managers. In fact, Zagallo lifted the World Cup twice as a player – in 1958 and 1962. Nice work.

Franz Beckenbauer

Mário Zagallo

TOP OF THE FLOPS

And now... here are the stories of three managers who had some decidedly low points in their managerial careers.

FOUL TEMPER

When Fiorentina player Adem Ljajic was substituted, in 2012, the sarcastic player pretended to applaud manager **Delio Rossi**'s decision. Rossi hit Ljajic and was soon unemployed.

SOLD OUT

In 2007, **Leroy Rosenior** was in charge of Torquay United for just ten minutes. As Rosenior was introducing himself at a press conference, the chairman stepped in to tell him the club had been sold and that he'd been sacked. That's surely the shortest management position in football history!

MISTAKEN IDENTITY

In 1996, Southampton manager **Graeme Souness** signed Senegalese footballer Ali Dia when Dia convinced him that he was the cousin of FIFA World Player of the Year George Weah. But Ali Dia was so poor in his only performance that his contract was cancelled. Oh, and he was no relation to Weah either!

OLD VS. YOUNG

One of the older managers on the scene is Brazilian **Luiz Felipe Scolari**, who was born in 1948. He led the Brazilian team to World Cup victory in 2002. He is still a head coach at the ripe old age of 66! Younger managers can be effective, too, bringing energy and fresh ideas. **Guy Roux** took over at Auxerre just before his 22nd birthday, in 1961. He kept the position for an amazing 44 years, bringing the French club many seasons of success.

TALKING TACTICS

Team tactics are all about player formations, set pieces, substitutions and split-second timing. The most successful teams can change their tactics to get the best out of every game. Some player formations were very popular in the past, but went out of favour when opposition teams learned how to deal with them...

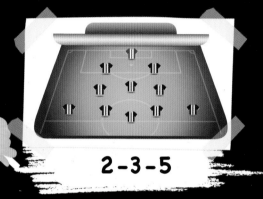

2-3-5

This system was used by most teams in the early 1900s. There were five attackers on the front line, made up of two wide players (wingers), two creative players (inside forwards) and one striker. There were also three midfielders and two defensive fullbacks.

4-2-4

In the 1950s, this formation brought great success to the Hungarian national team. They drew back one striker so that he played behind the other attackers, with a midfielder who moved around so that – at times – the formation shifted to 4–3–3 or 4–2–1–3.

4-4-2

The 4–4–2 was first used in the 1960s and is still incredibly popular today. When this formation goes on the attack, a defender or midfield player can join in with the strikers or even run beyond them towards the opposition's goal.

4-2-3-1

A popular modern formation is the 4–2–3–1. The two defensive midfield players usually play 'holding' roles to protect the defence. The three attacking midfielders try to join the main striker or run into gaps behind him or her when the team goes forwards.

TOP SECRET

Managers prefer to keep their tactics under wraps until kick-off. This gives them more chances to surprise the opposition in the fast-paced modern game. Here are some top tactics used to get the upper hand on the pitch...

CONFIDENTIAL

IN   **OUT**

OFF THE BENCH
FIFA introduced substitutions in 1923, so that injured players could be replaced. Today, teams use subs (up to three per competitive match) if a player is on a yellow card and running the risk of being sent off, if a player is tired and fresh legs are required, if a tactical or formation change is needed, or if the manager wants to rest an important player.

Pep Guardiola likes to use the 4–3–3, shifting it to a 4–1–4–1 formation at times.

SET PIECES
When they are training, teams work hard on set pieces, such as taking free kicks, corners and penalties. A well-practised set piece, a sudden run, lofty kick or split-second move can catch the opposition unawares and lead to a goal.

THE OFFSIDE TRAP
A clever but dangerous tactic is the 'offside trap'. An attacking player is offside if the ball is passed to them when there are fewer than two defenders (including the goalkeeper) between them and the opposite team's goal. Defenders can set the 'offside trap' by pulling right back from their goal, making an opposing striker offside. If the trap is set successfully, the defence gets an indirect free kick. If not, the striker has an almost clear run at the goal!

PLAY LIKE THE PROS

It's all very well watching the game's grand masters showing off their trick shots all over the pitch – but for us ordinary mortals, only practice makes perfect. Here are some top tips on how to perform the most eye-popping, jaw-dropping moves so you can play like a professional... or at least impress your mates!

THE PANENKA PENALTY

Czech penalty-taker **Antonín Panenka** showed nerves of steel when faced with a possible winner in a shootout at the European Championship final of 1976. Instead of blasting the ball left or right, he calmly chipped it over the diving West German keeper... into the back of the net.

1 Approach the ball as if to take a normal penalty.

2 At the last second, chip the ball high into the middle of the goal as if there was no keeper.

3 Hope the goalkeeper has dived one way or the other, leaving an empty net for the goal.

THE CRUYFF TURN

This piece of magic came to the world's attention when Dutch hot-shot **Johan Cruyff** displayed it at the World Cup in 1974 (held in West Germany). It's a great tactic to use when you need to ditch an opponent as quick as you can.

1 Get the ball in between your feet.

2 Flick the ball with the inside of one foot so it goes behind the standing leg, in the opposite direction from the way you're facing.

WOW!!

3 Turn to face the opposite direction and speed away.

RADICAL RABONA

Tottenham Hotspur striker **Erik Lamela** famously used the 'rabona' technique to score during a 2014 Europa League match against Greek side Asteras Tripolis. The technique was first seen in Spain – and, for no obvious reason, is named after the Argentinian word meaning 'to skip school'! For more obvious reasons, it is sometimes called a 'cross-kick'.

1 As you approach the ball, place your non-kicking leg on the opposite side of the ball. For example: if you are right-footed, place your left leg on the right-hand side of the ball.

2 Swing at the ball with your kicking leg from behind the standing leg.

SUPER STEP-OVER TURNS

This smooth move was developed in the 1920s and brought to the big stage by star players of the modern game, such as **Ronaldinho** and **Ronaldo**. A number of misleading step-over turns can confuse opponents. As each defender is sent the wrong way, the player on the ball is given more time.

Genius!

1 Lift one foot over or around the ball so that both feet are on the same side of it.

2 Drop one shoulder, shift your bodyweight and use either foot to move the ball away from the defender. Accelerate away.

HAIR-RAISERS

Televized games and internet highlights have turned players into global style icons. Strips and boots are more and more colourful and eye-catching, while crazy hairstyles are cut and clipped throughout the season... almost as often as a football pitch!

BLOND BOMBSHELL

Like a pirate plundering the high seas, the bearded French striker **Djibril Cissé** tore apart defences. But this was no Blackbeard. To match his canary yellow hair, he put peroxide on his facial hair. Ta-dah! Blondbeard was born.

MEGA MULLETS

The 1980s were a time of neon socks, shoulder pads and 'mullet' hairstyles. **Chris Waddle**'s highlighted mullet cascaded around his shoulders, but thankfully it disappeared when the decade passed. Phew!

DYED DREADS

Dreadlocks look super funky and are well worked by South African star and Everton winger **Steven Pienaar**. But Inter Milan's **Taribo West** took the style further! His dreads were vibrant green, and he stuck with this look through most of the 1990s and 2000s.

GOLDILOCKS

Colombia's **Carlos Valderrama** appeared to play under a golden halo in the 1990s. His huge, dyed Afro hairstyle brought him worldwide recognition. There was no need for a numbered shirt when you could spot him a mile off!

TINY TUFT

During the 2002 World Cup, Brazilian belter **Ronaldo** modelled a shaved head except for a little tuft on top. His fans were left wondering what on earth 'the Phenomenon' was thinking. But when you're three times World Footballer of the Year, success must go to your head!

THE DIVINE PONYTAIL

During the 1980s and '90s, Italian legend **Roberto Baggio** sported a hairstyle that must have looked better in his mirror than it did on the pitch. His plaited ponytail and messy mullet earned him the nickname *Il Divin Codinio* (The Divine Ponytail).

FRED THE RED

Swedish winger **Freddie Ljungberg** showed his team's colours by dyeing his hair bright red while playing for Arsenal in 2002. He experimented with colours for a while, then shaved it all off.

SUPER MARIO

Italian ball-blaster **Mario Balotelli** is often seen with a multicoloured Mohawk of white, yellow or black. It is sometimes accompanied by striking patterns shaved into both sides of his head.

HAIR TODAY, GONE TOMORROW

Trendsetter **David Beckham** is a global style icon who has been picked to advertise many big brands. Throughout his career, his hairstyles changed like the wind – including bleached blond, spiky, Mohican, mullet, high ponytail, cornrows and skinhead.

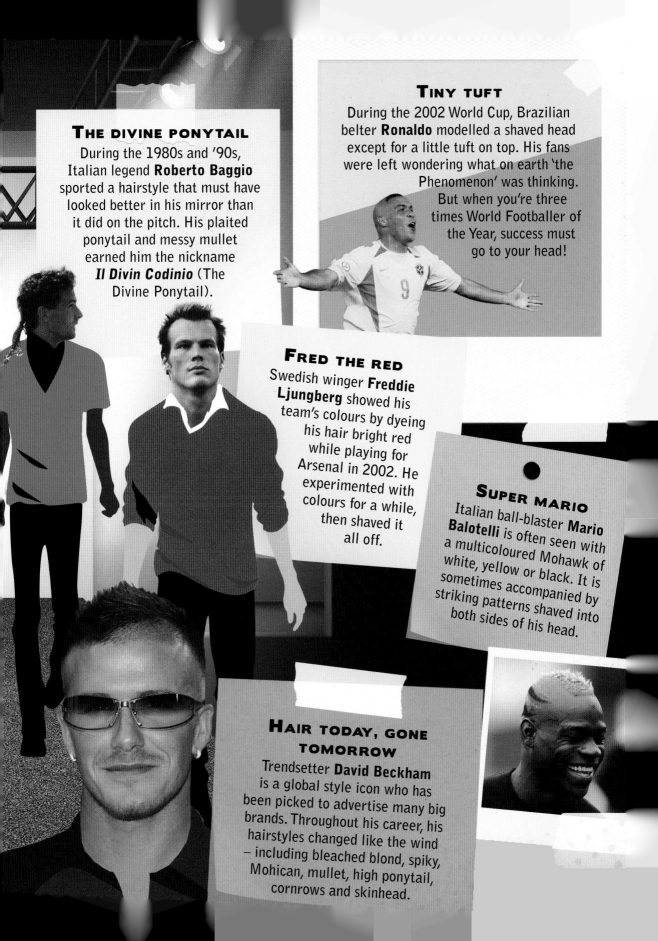

GOAL MACHINES

It is the striker's job to score – and if a forward is on good form, the goals can fly in from anywhere. Headers, long shots, tap-ins and set pieces all hit the back of the net. As the goals pile up, players can become legends for their clubs.

LUCKY 13

Australia beat American Samoa 31–0 in a qualifier for the 2002 World Cup. This was the biggest win ever in an international football match, but one player on the pitch made his own piece of history. **Archie Thompson** broke the record for most goals scored in a single game, hammering 13 past the opposition.

0.97 GOALS PER GAME

HUNGARY FOR GOALS

Ferenc Puskás scored big for his clubs Real Madrid and Budapest Honvéd. In 529 league games, the Hungarian striker scored 514 goals! He helped his national team to win the 1952 Olympics and also reached the 1954 World Cup final.

FERNANDO ON FIRE

Portuguese player **Fernando Peyroteo** had an incredible goal-scoring record. In 187 games for Sporting Lisbon in the 1930s and '40s, he racked up 331 goals – an average of nearly two per game. In total, he scored 544 goals and was top scorer for his country a smashing six times.

BRAZILIAN BRILLIANCE

Pelé is famous for his incredible goal-scoring ability, but a less well-known Brazilian striker may have scored more. **Arthur Friedenreich** bagged an incredible 1,329 goals in 1,239 games between 1909 and 1935. Nicknamed the King of Football, this goal machine was Liga Paulista's leading scorer for nine seasons.

MESSI MASTERCLASS

Messi by name, meticulous by nature, the Barcelona frontman has a habit of breaking records. He scored 73 goals in one season alone for the Spanish champs, and – by the age of 28 – he'd already scored more than 400 goals for club and country. The top scorer ever in the Champions League, and with years left to play, Lionel Messi has plenty of time to set more records.

Number of goals

400 GOALS!!

400 · 300 · 200 · 100

2004 '05 '06 '07 '08 '09 '10 '11 '12 '13 '14 '15

GOAL DUDS!

Some strikers are unlucky – and this can really impact their career. When their confidence is crumbling and the fans are frustrated, these frontmen can grab the headlines for all the wrong reasons!

Liverpool thought they were getting a top deal when they signed Italian forward **Mario Balotelli** from AC Milan for £16 million in 2014, but they didn't get many goals banged in for their bucks. The striker scored only one goal in 16 appearances for Liverpool, who then loaned him to AC Milan.

Swedish striker **Marcus Berg** scored well at the 2009 Under-21s Euro Championships. German club Hamburger SV signed him and it took him less than three minutes to score on his debut. But then he managed only four goals in 30 games. He was loaned out to PSV Eindhoven, where he netted eight goals.

Great things were expected of Bulgarian striker **Valeri Bojinov** when he joined Manchester City in 2007. But it all went horribly wrong. After netting just one goal for the Sky Blues, he headed to Parma (in 2009) and then went from club to club in a string of fairly forgettable loans.

Mario Balotelli playing for Liverpool in 2015.

HAT-TRICK HEROES

Three is a magic number in football. Goals are great, but hat-tricks are better. A hat-trick is when one player scores three goals in a single match. This feat almost always guarantees the team a win. No wonder these hat-trick hotshots are the fans' favourites.

GOALS FOR KEEPS

There is only one professional goalkeeper who has netted a hat-trick in the history of football. As well as being great in goal, Paraguayan colossus **José Luis Chilavert** was a perfect penalty-taker for his Argentine club, Vélez, putting three of them past **Ferro Carril Oeste** in 1999.

José Luis Chilavert

Sadio Mané

2 MINS. 56 SECS

VILLA VICTOR

In 2015, Southampton striker **Sadio Mané** didn't waste any time when he netted three against Aston Villa in just 2 minutes and 56 seconds. The game finished 6–1, but it was the performance of the Senegalese star that will forever be remembered. His hat-trick is the fastest in the Premier League, setting a record that's unlikely to be broken.

CHANGING FACES

Despite being a defender, West Ham's **Alvin Martin** scored a hat-trick against Newcastle United in an 8–1 victory in 1986. But what made it unusual was that each of his goals beat a different keeper – **Martin Thomas** (who later went off injured), **Chris Hedworth** and **Peter Beardsley**. The faces changed, but the goals went past 'em all!

HURST'S HAT-TRICK

England fans hold 1966 close to their hearts, as it is the only time their national team won the World Cup, beating age-old rivals Germany 4–2 at Wembley Stadium. **Sir Geoff Hurst** netted three and remains the only player ever to have scored a hat-trick in a World Cup final.

Sir Geoff Hurst

HOTTER THAN A HAT-TRICK

For some strikers, getting a hat-trick is just not enough. As well as scoring 92 hat-tricks, Brazil's **Pelé** has scored five goals in a match on six occasions, and netted four goals at 30 different games.

Cristiano Ronaldo

Scored a hat-trick today

Scored a hat-trick today

MADRID'S MACHINE

Cristiano Ronaldo clearly wants to be known as King of the Hat-tricks. He has scored an astounding 27 hat-tricks for Real Madrid in La Liga (with two hat-tricks in four days!), which works out at more than four hat-tricks per season. He once grabbed five goals in a 9–1 battering of Granada in 2015.

GREATEST GOALS

If you ask any fan for their best football memory, it's usually a wonder goal. That unforgettable shot might be a super strike, a fancy flick or a terrific team effort. Here are some of the greatest goals ever seen.

MARCO VAN BASTEN
HOLLAND VS. USSR, EUROPEAN CHAMPIONSHIPS FINAL, 1988

In 1988, Holland won the Euro trophy thanks to a fantastic volley from **van Basten**. To the right of the penalty area, van Basten was on the receiving end of a cross from teammate **Arnold Muhren**. Despite the tight angle, van Basten took a risk, volleying the ball into the net.

DIEGO MARADONA
ARGENTINA VS. ENGLAND, WORLD CUP QUARTER-FINAL, 1986

No list of great goals would be complete without **Maradona**'s superb goal against England. Taking the ball from his own half of the pitch, the Argentine legend beat off four English players before kicking it past goalkeeper **Peter Shilton**.

RYAN GIGGS
MANCHESTER UNITED VS. ARSENAL, FA CUP SEMI-FINAL, 1999

This goal is often called the greatest in the history of the FA Cup. **Giggs** ran from his half of the pitch, bombing past player after player, before hammering the ball into the top of the net.

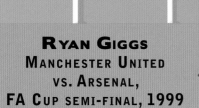

DENNIS BERGKAMP
HOLLAND VS. ARGENTINA, WORLD CUP QUARTER-FINAL, 1998

Receiving a great 50-yard pass from teammate **Ronald de Boer**, the dynamic Dutchman controlled the ball with three terrific touches before scoring the winner in the last moments of the game.

ZINEDINE ZIDANE
BAYER LEVERKUSEN VS. REAL MADRID, CHAMPIONS LEAGUE FINAL, 2002

The elegant French player scored one of the loveliest goals in the history of the Champions League. In the 45th minute, **Zidane** received a cross on the edge of the penalty area. Pirouetting smoothly, he sent a left-footed volley into the net.

WAYNE ROONEY
MANCHESTER UNITED VS. MANCHESTER CITY, PREMIER LEAGUE, 2011

Overhead kicks are **Rooney**'s speciality. His best shot came on the end of a cross from teammate **Nani**. Rooney thumped the ball into the top corner of the goal. This was voted the best Premier League goal in two decades.

MEGAN RAPINOE
USA VS. CANADA, OLYMPIC GAMES, 2012

Few goals go in from a corner because the angle is too tight, but US midfielder **Megan Rapinoe** (below right) made it look easy. Her curveball from the corner flag breezed past the post.

STEPHANIE ROCHE
PEAMOUNT UNITED VS. WEXFORD YOUTHS, WOMEN'S NATIONAL LEAGUE, 2013

In 2014, a woman was shortlisted for FIFA's Goal of the Year for the first time. It was thanks to a three-touch bombshell from Irish striker **Stephanie Roche.** Only a small crowd saw the goal live, but millions have since enjoyed it on the internet.

GAME OVER

In the days before most football grounds had undersoil heating, security systems or any of the mod cons, lots of matches were called off when weather or unexpected mishaps turned the pitch into a disaster area.

LIGHTNING STRIKERS
In 1998, a terrible thunderstorm in South Africa caused a match between Moroka Swallows and Jomo Cosmos to be abandoned. A lightning strike left three players unconscious, with two ending up in hospital.

POOCH ON THE PITCH
A dog interrupted a 1962 World Cup game between England and Brazil by running onto the pitch. He was on a mission to get the ball, as players tried in vain to stop his antics. Brazilian forward Garrincha was so smitten with the pooch that he kept him as a pet!

FROGS ON THE FIELD
Thousands of frogs took over a football pitch in Switzerland in 2015, leaving the referee no choice but to abandon the game. Embrach and Räterschen were drawing 2–2 in one of Zurich's amateur leagues when the croakers caused chaos.

NO-SHOW BLOW

A World Cup qualifier between Scotland and Estonia was set for 6.45 p.m. on 9 October 1996. The match was moved earlier, to 9 a.m., because the floodlights were broken. Estonia said they had not been given enough time, so they didn't turn up. The Scots kicked off without any opposition. FIFA ordered the match to be replayed and the result was a goalless draw!

BROLLY WALLY

Legend has it that Aston Villa winger **Charlie Athersmith** took matters into his own hands when rain began hammering down on a match against Sheffield United in 1901. He decided to play the second half holding an umbrella he borrowed from a spectator.

SLOG IN THE FOG

One match that should have been called off but went ahead anyway was Arsenal against Dynamo Moscow in 1945. The fog was so thick that the fans couldn't see the game, and both teams sneaked on an extra player because the referee couldn't tell how many were on the pitch!

BOMBS AWAY

In 1985, Sheffield United learned their club was near the site of a huge, unexploded World War II bomb. A match against Oldham had to be delayed while the bomb was defused.

FAMOUS FOES

A bit of friendly rivalry never hurt anyone, but these famous foes are anything but friendly. Some conflicts are between the giants of the footballing world. Others are between little local sides. Whatever the reason, when the two teams go head to head, it's unmissable.

BARCELONA VS. REAL MADRID

When Spanish teams Barcelona and Real Madrid play each other in their El Clásico derbies, it's a chance to watch the world's best footballing talent. The teams first met in 1902, when Barça won 3–1. Today Barcelona's line-up is led by **Lionel Messi**, while **Cristiano Ronaldo** puts his best foot forward for Madrid.

Lionel Messi

Cristiano Ronaldo

AC MILAN VS. INTER MILAN

AC Milan and Inter Milan are known as Italy's feuding cousins. The Milan cricket and football club (AC Milan) was established by an Englishman in 1899, before a team of Italian and Swiss players (Inter Milan) was set up in 1908. Though the fans' loyalties divide the city, the clubs share the spectacular San Siro stadium.

Luiz Adriano

Mauro Icardi

RIVER PLATE VS. BOCA JUNIORS

The city of Buenos Aires, in Argentina, comes to a standstill when these two local teams take each other on. Boca Juniors come from a poor part of town, while the River Plate team moved to a wealthy suburb, resulting in their nickname, 'Los Millonarios'. The two sets of fans compete to cheer loudest.

Enzo Francescoli

Juan Ramán Riquelme

GALATASARAY VS. FENERBAHÇE

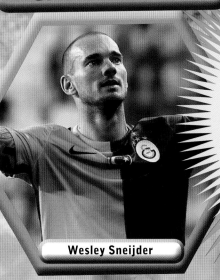

The city of Istanbul is split by the water of the Bosphorus Straits: Galatasaray is in the European part, while Fenerbahçe is in Asia. Galatasaray are often the victors. Their manager **Graeme Souness** stirred up yet more tension in 1996 by sticking his club's flag in Fenerbahçe's pitch after his side won!

Wesley Sneijder

Nani

MANCHESTER UTD VS. LIVERPOOL

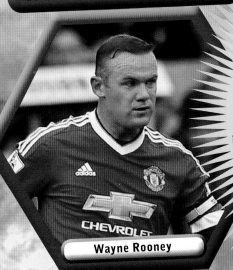

Manchester United and Liverpool are firm foes. The pair have 18 league wins each. In head-to-head matches, Manchester are in the lead with 77 wins to 64. The pair first met in an FA Cup final in 1977. Liverpool's hopes were high, having just won the league. Those hopes were cruelly dashed when Manchester grabbed the cup with a 2–1 win.

Wayne Rooney

Daniel Sturridge

OPEN YOUR EYES, REF

Football referees must control the match calmly and fairly. They must step in only when necessary. As well as knowing the rules inside out, they must be fit to keep up with the fast-moving players. If a ref ticks all these boxes, it's game on!

MATCH-DAY ESSENTIALS

The referee carries a whistle, which is blown to start and stop play. Yellow and red cards are used to book and send off players. A notepad and pen are used to record the names of booked players. A special FIFA coin is flipped to determine the team that will kick off the game and the direction they will play. Until the mid-1990s, referees dressed entirely in black. Today, FIFA allows refs a choice of black, red, yellow, green or blue jersey.

THE FIRST REFEREES

Back in the 19th century, amateur clubs brought their own umpires to watch games. But these umpires were always likely to favour their own team, so it was never really fair! In 1891, the first referee with no ties to either team was brought on to the pitch. The umpires were made linesmen, now known as assistant referees. The first woman to referee a men's English Football League match was **Amy Fearn** in 2010. Female referees for men's professional matches are on the rise across the world.

REFEREE SIGNALS

Referees must make themselves understood, despite all the crowd noise and players shouting. They often do this using signs and gestures:

Amy Fearn

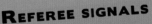

Direction of throw-in

Direct free kick

Red card sending off

> The ref often takes the blame from the fans if their team is doing badly. But when decisions must be made in a second, mistakes can happen!

HAND OF GOD

England fans will never forget Argentinian player **Diego Maradona** scoring against them in the 1986 World Cup quarter-finals – with a handball! Maradona himself later admitted he'd had some help from 'the hand of God'. Referee **Ali Bin Nasser** gave the goal and the game finished 2–1 to Argentina, who went on to win the competition.

Maradona's 'Hand of God'

CARD CHAOS

In 2009, a Spanish match between Recreativo Linense and Saladillo de Algeciras turned into a brawl and the game was called off. Referee **Jose Manuel Barro Escandón** followed the players into the changing rooms and gave out 19 red cards!

LOST COUNT

Referee **Graham Poll** lost count of his yellow cards when Croatia played Australia in 2006. **Josip Simunic** was in luck when he received three yellow cards before finally being given the red that sent him off the pitch.

Graham Poll

JAW DROPPER

During a 1982 match between France and Germany, German goalkeeper **Harald Schumacher** threw himself at French forward **Patrick Battiston** so hard that he knocked him unconscious. With a broken jaw and missing three teeth, Battiston was carried off. Referee **Charles Korver** gave a goal kick to Germany!

GREAT GOALIES!

Behind every great club is a solid defence, headed up by a gutsy goalkeeper. A fantastic performance by a great goalie can result in 'clean sheets' – games in which no goals are scored against the team. Here are some of the ultimate heroes in goal.

Italian keeper **Gianluigi Buffon** is considered one of the greatest goalies of all time. He broke the record for a goalkeeper's transfer fee when Juventus signed him from Parma for an eye-watering £33 million in 2001.

São Paulo captain and goalkeeper **Rogério Ceni**'s free kicks and penalty strikes have netted 140 goals for his club. This makes him the top-scoring goalkeeper in the history of football, putting many strikers to shame.

In 1977–78, Brazilian keeper **Matos Mazarópi** was in goal for Vasco de Gama for 1,816 minutes without letting any balls past him. At the other end of the scale is American Samoa's **Nicky Salapu**, who let 31 goals slip past in a single World Cup qualifier against Australia in 2001.

Gordon Banks watches the ball fly past the post after his amazing save.

Poor Nicky Salapu lets in another goal.

Lots of fans think the save of the century was when **Gordon Banks** pushed out Brazilian striker **Pele**'s header during the 1970 World Cup. It looked unstoppable!

CRAZY KEEPERS

It's a stressful, lonely job being a goalkeeper, which may explain why a few have had some unusual habits.

Early 20th-century Welsh goalie **Leigh Richmond Roose** always wore the same lucky vest under his shirt – and never washed it, much to the horror of his teammates.

In the 19th century, English goalkeeper **Jack Robinson** chomped his way through a plate of rice pudding before every game. He claimed it brought him good luck. On the one occasion he skipped his snack, he let in 11 goals.

Bruce Grobbelaar was an expert at putting players off penalties. In goal for Liverpool against Roma in the 1984 European Cup final, he distracted one penalty-taker by wobbling his legs at them. He confused another by attempting to eat the goal net.

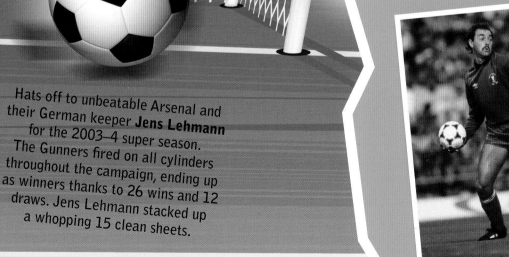

Hats off to unbeatable Arsenal and their German keeper **Jens Lehmann** for the 2003–4 super season. The Gunners fired on all cylinders throughout the campaign, ending up as winners thanks to 26 wins and 12 draws. Jens Lehmann stacked up a whopping 15 clean sheets.

Bruce Grobbelaar throws in during the 1984 European Cup final.

WINNING WOMEN

Women have been playing football for as long as the game has existed, but the 21st century has seen the start of an exciting new era. Today, women's football has international tournaments, huge sponsorship deals and wide TV coverage. Girls are giving the boys a run for their money!

STEP BY STEP

1895 One of the first official women's matches takes place, between the North of England and the South of England.

1920 The first women's international match is played, between Dick, Kerr Ladies of Preston, England, and a team from Paris, France. They are watched by a crowd of 25,000.

1921 There are around 150 women's teams in England, but the English Football Association bans ladies playing on league grounds because: "The game of football is quite unsuitable for females and ought not to be encouraged." The ban is not lifted until 1971!

1970s The first part-time professional women's league is set up in Italy. Other countries follow their example.

1991 The first FIFA Women's World Cup tournament is held. It is won by the United States.

1996 A women's football tournament is staged at the Olympics for the first time.

2001 The UEFA Women's Champions League tournament begins. It is won by FFC Frankfurt.

TOP LEAGUE TEAMS

Lauren Holiday (left) of Kansas City kicks the ball away from Jessica Fishlock of Seattle Reign.

KANSAS CITY

Kansas City, one of the most successful women's teams in the USA, won the 2014 National Women's Soccer League. The team was only founded in 2012. Players **Becky Sauerbrunn**, **Heather O'Reilly**, **Lauren Holiday** and **Amy Rodriguez** are also in the national team.

GIRL POWER IN NUMBERS

30 MILLION

45 MILLION

FIFA hopes to expand the number of female football players worldwide from **30 TO 45 MILLION** for the 2019 World Cup, which will take place in France.

51 countries have a women's national football league.

At least **400 MILLION** viewers watched the 2011 Women's World Cup in Germany.

The 2015 Women's World Cup final was the most watched football game ever on US TV, with **25.4 MILLION VIEWERS.**

ARSENAL LFC

Arsenal Ladies Football Club is the most successful English women's team and winner of the UEFA Women's Champions League in 2007. Star players include **Kelly Smith**, who is the England national team's top scorer, with 46 goals for her country.

Kelly Smith

FFC FRANKFURT

This German women's Bundesliga team have won the UEFA Women's Champions League a total of four times. They are locked in a friendly rivalry with 1 FFC Turbine Potsdam, another Bundesliga team. A former star Frankfurt player is **Birgit Prinz**, three-time FIFA World Player of the Year.

FFC Frankfurt win the Champions League in 2015.

A NUMBERS GAME...

All eyes on the pitch for the second half of our run-down of the most fantastic footballing statistics, scores and sums. Watch out for the fastest goal, the highest score and the longest winning streak.

£84,000,000

LEG WORK

Gareth Bale's legs are insured for a whopping £84 million by Real Madrid. Like his teammate Cristiano Ronaldo, Bale's legs are insured for a record-breaking sum to protect against him suffering a serious injury.

106

WINNING STREAK

Romanian club Steaua Bucureşti went unbeaten for 106 games from 1986 to 1989. During that time, the high fliers won five consecutive titles.

GOAL BONANZA

Brazil's Ronaldinho scored 23 goals in a youth team match aged just 13, making the score 23–0. He went on to win the World Cup in 2002 and the Champions League with Barcelona in 2006.

23

STAND-OUT SCORE

The highest-ever score in a World Cup final was 10–1, when Hungary hammered El Salvador in 1982. During the match, László Kiss became the first substitute to score a hat-trick in a World Cup match.

WEIGHT OF THE WORLD

6 KG

The World Cup trophy is a weighty 6 kilograms. The current trophy has been used since 1974. Football's greatest prize stands 36 centimetres tall and is made of 18 carat gold.

SEPTEMBER, 2010

57 HOURS

1	2	3	4	5	6	7
8	9	10	11	12	13	14
15	16	17	18	19	20	21
22	23	24	25	26	27	28
29	30					

MARATHON MATCH

The longest match in football history was 57 hours. In 2010, the match between Leeds Badgers and Warwickshire Wolves went on for more than two days and two nights, with a jaw-dropping final score of 425–354. The teams were trying to create a new world record and raise loads of money for charity – and they were winners on both counts!

QUICK OFF THE MARK

The fastest goal ever scored in a World Cup match was scored just 10 seconds into the game. In 2002, Turkey's **Hakan Sükür** zipped the ball into the South Korean net just moments after kick-off.

35.1 kph

FAST FORWARD

The top speed of the fastest player in the world is 35.1 kilometres per hour. A study by FIFA revealed that Manchester United's **Antonio Valencia** is fastest on his feet.

33

CUP CANCELLATIONS

In the winter season of 1963, a game was postponed 33 times. This Scottish cup tie between Stranraer and Airdrie was rearranged and cancelled again and again because of freezing temperatures and an icy pitch.

10

RECORD-BREAKING CHAMPIONS

Real Madrid has won the Champions League 10 times, making them the most successful club in the tournament's history.

MEMORABLE MATCHES

Once seen, some games can never be forgotten. These headline-grabbing matches are famous for their sky-high score, jaw-dropping result or last-minute victory.

One of the greatest games ever seen was when Real Madrid battled Eintracht Frankfurt in the 1960 European Cup final. There were 120,000 fans in the stadium and millions of television viewers. The Germans scored first, despite Real having more opportunities. But early in the second half, Real were leading 5–1. Suddenly, in the most extraordinary four minutes of football, both teams scored twice! Of Real's seven goals, Ferenc Puskás netted four and Alfredo Di Stéfano scored a hat trick.

REAL MADRID 7 EINTRACHT FRANKFURT 3

18 MAY 1960
HAMPDEN PARK STADIUM, GLASGOW, SCOTLAND

Eintracht's Richard Kress score the first goal of the match.

Brazilian player Maicon tries to cheer up teammate Luiz Gustavo.

BRAZIL 1 GERMANY 7

9 JULY 2014
ARENA DE SAO PAULO, BRAZIL

What a shocker! World Cup host nation Brazil thought their team would race home to victory in the semi-final with Germany, even though they were playing without superstar Neymar and captain Thiago Silva. All hope was lost within half an hour, when Germany were leading 5–0. There was only despair to come in the second half when Germany got another two in the net, before Brazil's last-minute goal. This devastating defeat was the first competitive home game that Brazil had lost in 39 years and the biggest World Cup semi-final thrashing ever.

LIVERPOOL 0
ARSENAL 2

26 MAY 1989
ANFIELD, LIVERPOOL,
ENGLAND

AIR MAIL
PAR AVION

FA Cup winners Liverpool were top of the league and favourites to keep the league title in the last game of the season, against the Gunners, at Liverpool's home ground. Second place Arsenal had to win by two clear goals to top the league, a defeat Liverpool hadn't experienced at home for three years. The visitors scored early in the second half, leaving the game on a knife-edge. In the last minute, Arsenal's Michael Thomas flicked the ball into the net, winning Arsenal the league. You should have heard the crowd roar!

Michael Thomas scores in the final minute!

Milan were hot favourites to win the UEFA Champions League final against Liverpool, but nothing turned out like expected! By half-time, Milan had scored three goals while Liverpool had scored... none. In an extraordinary second half, Liverpool netted three goals in six minutes to level the scores at 3–3. There were no more goals in extra time, so a nail-biting penalty shootout was needed to decide the winners – leaving the score 3–2 to Liverpool. Everyone was soon calling the match the Miracle of Istanbul!

AC MILAN 3
LIVERPOOL 3
(LIVERPOOL WON
3–2 ON PENALTIES)

25 MAY 2005
ATATÜRK STADIUM,
ISTANBUL, TURKEY

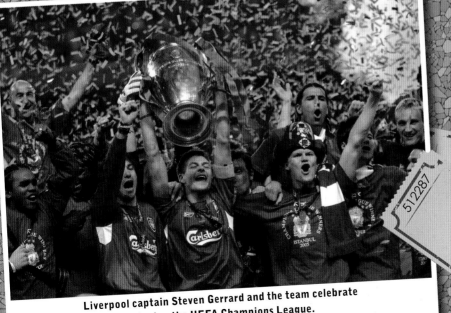

Liverpool captain Steven Gerrard and the team celebrate winning the UEFA Champions League.

EURO CHAMPIONS!

UEFA CHAMPIONS LEAGUE WINNERS

1955–60	REAL MADRID
1960–62	BENFICA
1962–63	AC MILAN
1963–65	INTERNAZIONALE
1965–66	REAL MADRID
1966–67	CELTIC
1967–68	MANCHESTER UNITED
1968–69	AC MILAN
1969–70	FEYENOORD
1970–73	AJAX
1973–76	BAYERN MUNICH
1976–78	LIVERPOOL
1978–80	NOTTINGHAM FOREST
1980–81	LIVERPOOL
1981–82	ASTON VILLA
1982–83	HAMBURG
1983–84	LIVERPOOL
1984–85	JUVENTUS
1985–86	STEAUA BUCURESTI
1986–87	PORTO
1987–88	PSV EINDHOVEN
1988–90	AC MILAN
1990–91	RED STAR BELGRADE
1991–92	BARCELONA
1992–93	MARSEILLE
1993–94	AC MILAN
1994–95	AJAX

The world's biggest club competition is the UEFA Champions League, which was called the European Cup until 1992. Every season, the tournament gives us wonder goals, nail-biting moments and top teamwork.

GET REAL!

We can't talk about the Champions League without mentioning Real Madrid. When the competition started in 1955, Real won the first five seasons, a record that no other club has come close to beating. They also won in 2014, when goals from **Cristiano Ronaldo**, **Gareth Bale**, **Marcelo** and **Sergio Ramos** gave them a 4–1 win over Atlético Madrid. This was Real Madrid's tenth European Cup.

The top goal-scorers in the competition are **Lionel Messi** and **Cristiano Ronaldo**, who both boast 77 goals.

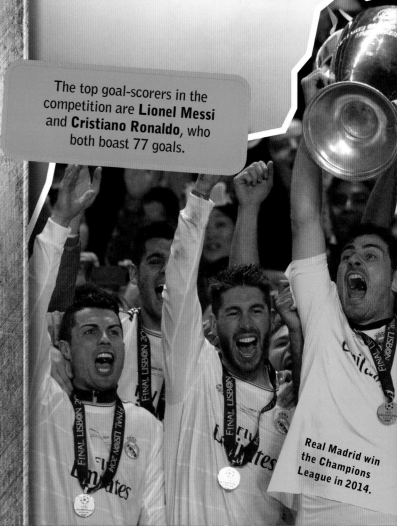

Real Madrid win the Champions League in 2014.

MOST GOALS

In 1965–66, Benfica beat Luxembourg's Stade Dudelange 8–0 and 10–0. However, the biggest win in a single match is awarded to Dutch team Feyenoord, who scored 12 past KR Reykjavík in 1970. The Icelanders mustered up two goals in response.

Feyenoord took the European Cup in 1970.

BETTER LATE THAN NEVER

Manchester United left it very late in the 1999 final against Bayern Munich. For most of the game, the Red Devils were trailing 1–0, but two goals in the last minutes of injury time saw them lift the trophy. Celebrated referee **Pierluigi Collina** said the noise in the stadium was like a 'lion's roar' when **Ole Gunnar Solskjær** scored the winner.

1995–96	**JUVENTUS**
1996–97	**BORUSSIA DORTMUND**
1997–98	**REAL MADRID**
1998–99	**MANCHESTER UNITED**
1999–2000	**REAL MADRID**
2000–01	**BAYERN MUNICH**
2001–02	**REAL MADRID**
2002–03	**AC MILAN**
2003–04	**PORTO**
2004–05	**LIVERPOOL**
2005–06	**BARCELONA**
2006–07	**AC MILAN**
2007–08	**MANCHESTER UNITED**
2008–09	**BARCELONA**
2009–10	**INTERNAZIONALE**
2010–11	**BARCELONA**
2011–12	**CHELSEA**
2012–13	**BAYERN MUNICH**
2013–14	**REAL MADRID**
2014–15	**BARCELONA**

Dutch midfielder **Clarence Seedorf** has won the Champions League four times, playing for a record three different clubs: Ajax, AC Milan and Real Madrid.

FOOTBALL FIESTA

South America is a continent that celebrates football in style. With a carnival atmosphere in the stadiums, spectators turn great games into pitch-side parties. At the heart of the action is the coveted Copa América, the world's oldest international competition.

SOUTH AMERICA'S TOP TEAMS

The Brazil team of 1970 is legendary.

BRILLIANT BRAZIL

On the world stage, Brazil has enjoyed supreme success. With an extraordinary five wins, they have lifted the World Cup trophy more times than any other nation. It is often said that the best team ever to play in a World Cup were the Brazilian legends who beat Italy 4–1 in the 1970 final. That team was captained by **Carlos Alberto** and included **Pelé**, **Gérson**, **Jairzinho**, **Rivellino** and **Tostão**. The Brazilian women's team has won the Copa América Femenina six times out of the seven times the tournament has taken place.

Copa América wins: 8
Today's star players: Neymar (forward/winger), Ramires (attacking midfielder), Robinho (forward)
Top clubs in the Brazilian league: Santos, Palmeiras, Cruzeiro

Chile won the Copa América in 2015.

THE COPA AMÉRICA

The ten members of the South American Football Confederation (CONMEBOL) compete in the Copa América: Argentina, Bolivia, Brazil, Chile, Colombia, Ecuador, Paraguay, Peru, Uruguay and Venezuela. They are always joined by two guest teams, usually from North or Central America or the Caribbean. With 15 wins, Uruguay has lifted the trophy the most times. Ecuador and Venezuela are the only South American teams never to win. In 2016, it is 100 years since the first competition.

YOU'RE GREAT URUGUAY!

This tiny nation, with a population of just 3.3 million, is the smallest country in the world to have won the World Cup, in 1930 and 1950. It has also won gold at the Olympic Games twice. In fact, Uruguay holds the world record for the most international titles held by any country: 20.

Copa América wins: 15
Today's star players: Luis Suárez (striker), Edinson Cavani (forward), Egidio Arévalo (defensive midfielder)
Top clubs in the Uruguayan league: Peñarol, Nacional

AWESOME ARGENTINA

Argentina has won the World Cup twice, in 1978, when they hosted, and in 1986. The nation has produced a host of players considered to be all-time greats, including **Diego Maradona** and **Javier Zanetti**, with 147 caps for his country. Today's superstar has to be **Lionel Messi.** He joined Barcelona aged 11, after the club agreed to pay for the growth hormone treatment he needed.

Copa América wins: 14
Today's star players: Lionel Messi (forward), Carlos Tevez (forward), Javier Mascherano (midfielder/ defender), Sergio Agüero (striker)
Top clubs in the Argentinian league: River Plate, Boca Juniors, Racing

The Uruguay national team in 2014.

Argentina fans

TOP OF THE WORLD

The planet's biggest football competition is the FIFA World Cup, which takes place every four years. More than 200 national teams enter the qualifying rounds, but only the finest 32 make it to the final tournament.

HOSTS AND WINNERS

There have been twenty World Cup tournaments since the competition began in 1930. Only seven countries have ever won the cup. **Brazil** has won five World Cups and is the only nation to qualify for every tournament. **Italy** and **Germany** are the next biggest winners, with four cups each. **Argentina** and **Uruguay** have two each, while **England**, **France** and **Spain** have one each. The hosts of the competition (as well as the winners of the last competition) qualify automatically for the final stages of the tournament. In 2018, the host will be Russia.

HOSTS	WINNER	WORLD CUP FINAL SCORE
1930 URUGUAY	URUGUAY	URUGUAY 4–2 ARGENTINA
1934 ITALY	ITALY	ITALY 2–1 CZECHOSLOVAKIA
1938 FRANCE	ITALY	ITALY 4–2 HUNGARY
1942 NO COMPETITION DURING WORLD WAR II		
1946 NO COMPETITION DURING WORLD WAR II		
1950 BRAZIL	URUGUAY	URUGUAY 2–1 BRAZIL
1954 SWITZERLAND	GERMANY	GERMANY 3–2 HUNGARY
1958 SWEDEN	BRAZIL	BRAZIL 5–2 SWEDEN
1962 CHILE	BRAZIL	BRAZIL 3–1 CZECHOSLOVAKIA
1966 ENGLAND	ENGLAND	ENGLAND 4–2 GERMANY
1970 MEXICO	BRAZIL	BRAZIL 4–1 ITALY
1974 GERMANY	GERMANY	GERMANY 2–1 HOLLAND
1978 ARGENTINA	ARGENTINA	ARGENTINA 3–1 HOLLAND
1982 SPAIN	ITALY	ITALY 3–1 GERMANY
1986 MEXICO	ARGENTINA	ARGENTINA 3–2 GERMANY
1990 ITALY	GERMANY	GERMANY 1–0 ARGENTINA
1994 USA	BRAZIL	0–0 (ITALY LOST ON PENALTIES)
1998 FRANCE	FRANCE	FRANCE 3–0 BRAZIL
2002 JAPAN/ SOUTH KOREA	BRAZIL	BRAZIL 2–0 GERMANY
2006 GERMANY	ITALY	1–1 (FRANCE LOST ON PENALTIES)
2010 SOUTH AFRICA	SPAIN	SPAIN 1–0 NETHERLANDS
2014 BRAZIL	GERMANY	GERMANY 1–0 ARGENTINA

Top scorers

German legend **Miroslav Klose** is the top scorer in a World Cup career (2002, 2006, 2010, 2014), netting 16 goals overall.

Ronaldo comes second, with 15 goals in three tournaments (1998, 2002, 2006).

French forward **Just Fontaine** was the top goal-scorer in a single World Cup, in 1958. He hammered home 13 goals in six matches.

THE 2014 COMPETITION

The 20th tournament, held in Brazil, was the fifth time it has been held in South America. It was the first time that a European team has won a World Cup in the Americas. Germany defeated Argentina to lift the trophy. As always, the outstanding players were given awards: **Lionel Messi** (Argentina) won the Golden Ball, **Thomas Müller** (Germany) the Silver, and **Arjen Robben** (Netherlands) the Bronze.

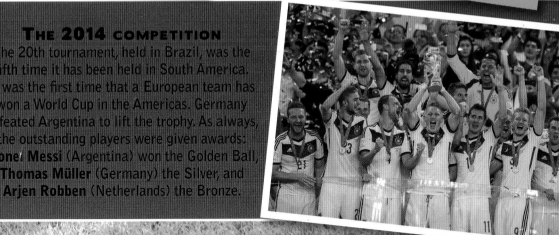

WEIRD AND WONDERFUL

A Brazilian player named **Vavá** experienced too much Va Va Voom when he scored against the Soviet Union in the 1958 World Cup. The rest of the team jumped on him, leaving him unconscious!

The World Cup trophy was stolen in 1966. It went missing while on display in London, England. Seven days later, a puppy called **Pickles** tracked it down. It was wrapped in newspaper and hidden in a hedge.

The Cup's youngest player was Northern Ireland's **Norman Whiteside**, who was 17 in 1982. The oldest goal-scorer was Cameroon's **Roger Milla**, who was 42 in 1994 when he scored against Russia.

IT'S A SHOOTOUT!

Nothing is more nail-biting than a penalty shootout. Trophies can be won or hearts broken by a single spot kick. While this method of deciding a result can be exciting to watch, the tension reaches fever pitch for the players and desperate fans.

PENALTY SHOOTOUT RULES

A penalty shootout takes place when a cup-tie has not been decided after 90 minutes plus extra time. Each of the chosen penalty-takers must shoot from the penalty spot, which is 11 metres from the goal line, with only the keeper to beat. Each team must take a minimum of five penalties. If the scores are still level, it goes to sudden death. No player can take a second penalty until the whole team has taken one.

Marco Materazzi shoots a penalty (and misses it) during the game Inter vs. Siena, in Italy 2008.

GOALIE GUESSES

The average penalty reaches 112 kilometres per hour, giving the goalie 700 milliseconds (7/10 of a second) to save the ball. But it takes almost a second to judge the direction of the kick and dive towards it. This means the keeper must move milliseconds before the player kicks the ball and try to predict the strike. Although the keeper is allowed to move, they must stay on the goal line until the ball is kicked.

MOST TWEETED

A penalty shootout at the 2014 World Cup in Brazil is the most tweeted-about moment of all time. On 28 June, messages on social networking site Twitter peaked at 389,000 per minute when Chilean player **Gonzalo Jara** missed his penalty, sending Brazil through to the quarter-finals.

Gonzalo Jara about to miss his penalty.

LONGEST SHOOTOUT

The record for the number of penalty kicks taken in a shootout is 48! That is how the 2005 Namibian Cup final was eventually settled, with KK Palace beating the Civics 17–16.

LETTING THE SIDE DOWN

The 2009–10 season fixture between Argentinian clubs Juventud Alianza and General Paz Juniors was a match the poor Alianza goalie will want to forget. This shootout ended 21–20, with the Alianza goalie failing to save any of the penalties!

SHOOTING SUCCESS

Attackers have a higher scoring success rate (86.7 per cent) than midfielders (79.6 per cent) and defenders (73.6 per cent).

UNDER PRESSURE!

Nerves affect a player's success! A player has a 93 per cent chance of scoring if the result will win a competition, but only 44 per cent if missing the penalty would see them lose the competition!

RULES OF THE GAME

 1: THE FIELD OF PLAY

The pitch must be between 90 and 120 metres long and 45 to 90 metres wide. Touchlines, sidelines, goal lines, goal areas, halfway line, centre circle, corner arcs, penalty areas, penalty arcs and penalty spots should be marked. A flag post should be on each corner of the field.

 2: THE BALL

The ball should have a diameter of 22 to 23 centimetres and weigh 400 to 450 grams.

 3: NUMBER OF PLAYERS

Matches must be played by two teams of between 7 and 11 players each, with one player per side as goalkeeper. In official competitions, only three substitutions are allowed.

 4: PLAYER'S KIT

Each player must wear a shirt, shorts, socks, shin guards and football boots. Goalkeepers should wear kit that distinguishes them from other players and the referees.

 5: HEAD REFEREE

A referee's job includes making sure that players obey the rules, signalling the start and end of the game, and stopping play if anyone needs medical attention.

6: ASSISTANT REFEREES

Assistant referees signal for corner kicks, throw-ins and offsides. They may draw any rule-breaking to the attention of the head referee.

7: LENGTH OF MATCH

A football match is 90 minutes, played in two halves of 45 minutes. Additional minutes, called 'injury period', may be played at the end of each half to make up for time lost. Overtime may be played in a competition if a winner is not decided after regular time.

 8: START AND RESTART OF PLAY

A kickoff starts a game and restarts it for the second half or after a goal is scored. A coin toss determines which team kicks off at the start of the match. During kickoff, only two players are allowed inside the centre circle: the one kicking and the one receiving the ball.

 9: BALL IN AND OUT OF PLAY

The ball is out of bounds if it crosses the goal line or touchline. If it bounces off a referee, goal post, crossbar or flag post and stays inside the field, it is still in play.

 10: SCORING

A goal is scored if the ball crosses the goal line between the goalposts and under the crossbar, as long as no rules have been broken. The side that scores the most goals wins. If both teams have the same number of goals (or no goals) at the end of a match, it is a draw.

11: OFFSIDE

A player is offside if the ball is played to them in the other team's half, unless at least two defenders (including the goalkeeper) are between the player and the goal. If a player is offside, an indirect free kick is given to the other team.

 12: FOULS AND MISCONDUCT

Fouls can be committed by a player while the ball is in play. Fouls include kicking, tripping or pushing another player recklessly; striking or trying to strike a member of the other team; deliberately handling the ball (unless the player is the goalkeeper in their area); using too much force while defending; and hitting the other player before the ball when tackling. Fouls are punished by a free kick or penalty kick to the other team. Misconduct is when a player commits repeated or serious fouls or when they behave in an unsporting way, whether or not the ball is in play. Misconduct is punished by a yellow card (for a caution) or a red card (for a sending off). Two yellow cards are the equivalent of a red card. A player who is sent off cannot be replaced.

 13: FREE KICKS

A free kick restarts play after a foul or other rule break. It is usually taken from the spot where the offence took place. A free kick can either be 'direct', when the kicker can score directly, or 'indirect', when another player must touch the ball before a goal can be scored. Indirect free kicks are awarded when the other team commits a less serious foul or goes offside.

14: PENALTY KICKS

A penalty kick is awarded if a defender commits a foul inside their own penalty area. The kick is taken from the penalty spot and all the players (except the kicker and goalkeeper) must be outside the penalty area and arc.

15: THROW-INS

If the ball goes over the touchline, a throw-in is awarded to the team opposing the side that touched the ball last. The throw is taken from the spot where the ball went out of bounds.

 16: GOAL KICKS

If the attacking team sends the ball over the goal line, a goal kick is awarded to the defending team. The ball must be kicked from the goal area and travel beyond the penalty area. The ball must be touched by another player before the kicker can play it again.

17: CORNER KICKS

If the defending team sends the ball over the goal line, a corner kick is awarded to the attacking team.

ASSISTANT REFEREE
Previously known as a linesman, an assistant referee is used on each side of the pitch to flag up offside decisions, fouls and throw-ins.

ATTENDANCE
The number of spectators at a football match.

CAP
Players keep count of their international matches in caps. In the past this was literally a hat given to players after an international game.

CHAMPIONS
The name given to the club that tops the league at the end of the football season.

CHIP
Looping the ball over the goalkeeper.

CLEAN SHEET
When a goalkeeper does not let in any goals.

CORNER
An advantageous way for the attacking team to restart the game when the ball has gone out of play behind the goal line after a touch from the last defender.

COUNTER-ATTACK
An attack on goal as a direct response to the other team's attempt to score.

DEFENDER
A role that involves working to stop the other team from scoring.

DISQUALIFICATION
A team's removal from a sporting competition for breaking the rules.

ENDORSEMENT
When a player is paid by a business to promote a product or item of clothing.

FORMATION
The manager's choice of how a team will line up and the tactics they will adopt across the field.

FORWARD
An attacking player responsible for scoring goals.

FULL BACK
Part of the defensive line, this player usually stays closer to the touchline, but often seeks to join or start attacks.

GIANT KILLER
When a lower division side beats a higher club against the odds.

HANDBALL
When a player's arms or hands touch the ball during play, unless the player is the keeper.

HAT-TRICK
The same player scoring three goals in a single match.

HEADER
When a player uses their head rather than their feet to make contact with the ball.

KICKABOUT
An informal and unplanned game of football.

LOAN
When a player is 'lent' to another club for a time.

MANAGER
The person in charge of picking, guiding and motivating the team.

MIDFIELDER
A player who uses the middle of the pitch to work defensively and creatively for the team.

PENALTY
An opportunity to score a goal from the penalty spot, following an offence by the other team in the penalty area.

PROFESSIONAL
A person who earns their living from playing football.

QUALIFIER
A match played in order to gain entry to a major competition.

REPLAY
An extra match played to decide the winning team, if a cup game ends in a draw.

SET PIECE
A way of restarting the game after a foul, when the ball has gone out of play, or a goal has been scored.

SHOOTOUT
If two teams are drawing after extra time in a cup game, a penalty shootout decides the winner.

SHOWBOAT
A player showing off special skills on the ball.

SPONSORSHIP
When a business pays a player or team in return for their name being on the team's kit, for example.

STOPPAGE TIME
Time added on to each half of a match by the referee. Time is added for stops in play caused by injuries, goal celebrations, substitutions and timewasting.

STRIKER
A forward responsible for scoring goals.

STUDS
Knobs on the sole of a football boot to aid grip and balance on the pitch.

SUBSTITUTE
A player brought on from the bench to replace a player already on the pitch.

TACTICS
A team's pre-planned ideas and actions to beat the other team.

TRANSFER
The movement of a player from one club to another, usually involving a payment if the player is still under contract with the selling club.

UNDERDOG
A team considered weaker than the team they are playing, because of their league standing or standard of play.

VOLLEY
When a ball is kicked while it is still in the air, before it touches the ground.

WINGER
A striker who makes runs down one side of the pitch to create chances.

PICTURE CREDITS